CORKSCREW SOLUTIONS

PROBLEM SOLVING WITH A TWIST

CLARKE CHING

INTRODUCTION - PUZZLES

"A pessimist sees the difficulty in every opportunity;
an optimist sees the opportunity in every difficulty."
– A quote never said by Winston Churchill

Way back in the late 1970s, when I was 10 years old, I got stuck for weeks trying to solve a particularly tricky puzzle called the *Nine Dots Puzzle*.

Here are the instructions if you'd like to give it a go:

- Find a blank piece of paper and a pen.
- Draw 9 dots on the paper, in 3 equally spaced rows of 3 dots.

Like this:

- Now use the pen to connect all 9 dots by drawing 4 straight lines without lifting the pen from the paper.

Here's a failed attempt:

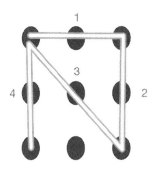

- Keep trying, drawing as quickly as you can.
- Don't give up—ever—until you've solved it!

Try solving the puzzle now. Give it a couple of shots. I'll wait.

———

It took me 25 years to solve this puzzle.

To be fair, most of that effort happened during the two or three weeks after I first bumped into it. I kept trying and trying and then trying some more to solve it. Drawing it on paper at first, then, once I got the hang of things, I started trying to solve it in my head. I ran scenario after scenario, constantly failing until eventually, I gave up.

I stumbled across the 9-dots puzzle again when I was in my late 30s.

I was attending a course about creativity.

The trainer kicked off a session on what he called, 'Out of the Box Thinking.'

That's the kind of thinking you're supposed to do when your current thinking isn't working.

He drew out the 9 dots, explained the puzzle's rules and then asked us to solve it.

We started scribbling and then a few minutes later he stopped us.

He said, "This puzzle is impossible . . ."

I imagine we all reacted the same way—with a face that resembled this 😵 or this 😲 emoji.

He smiled, he taught this course several times a year and that was the exact reaction he expected.

He took a moment giving us time to recover before he said, "Yeah, it's impossible . . . unless you know the trick."

I guess we all probably pulled a bunch of different faces ranging from surprised to enlightened.

I remember feeling angry. Not at him. Not at the puzzle. But at whoever invented the puzzle for not pointing out to geeky, naive 10-year-old me that there was a trick.

My thoughts went something like this:

```
There's a trick?
No, there can't be.
```

```
That'd just be mean.
```

And then I looked at the title of the session: 'Out of the Box Thinking' . . . and I got it!

```
OMG. OMG. OMG.
There's a %%%^&&$$% trick.
You can draw outside the %%%^&&$$%
box.
```

The trainer confirmed what I had just thought: "You can draw outside the lines."

And then he showed us, 'Like this.'

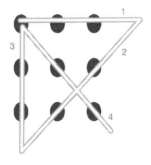

I had one of those slap-your-forehead 'Doh!' moments when you realize something is so obvious that you can't believe you missed it and didn't see it before. And now you can never not see it again.

I'd *assumed* you had to draw only inside the grid. You could say that I invented that *rule*. It certainly wasn't actually part of the rules.

Doh!

The trainer explained that this puzzle was, in fact, where the expression to *think outside the box* came from.

It's good advice but only because it forces you to pause and ask yourself: do we need to try something different?

It would be better advice if it taught us how—if it taught us the trick.

———

This book will teach you two tricks.

All great leaders and thinkers use these two tricks to solve seemingly impossible real-world problems. Soon you will too.

PART 1

WINSTON CHURCHILL
WORLD WAR ONE

CHAPTER 1

KILLER DUCKLINGS

It's 1999 and I'm sitting next to my wife in a hotel ballroom in her hometown, Kilkenny, Ireland. We're at a wedding reception, it's a big reception because the bride has 87 cousins. We're sitting at the head table at the front of the ballroom facing out towards the guests. Our parents are sitting at the table too. Her parents drove 7 minutes to get there. My mum and dad flew over from New Zealand. My wife and I were married a few hours earlier.

We're all sitting there, and we have a problem . . . or rather a potential problem.

My dad, a gnarly, sun-beaten New Zealand farmer who always spoke in his 'outdoor voice' no matter whether he was inside or out, one of life's conversational wild cards . . . has somehow ended up sitting beside the priest.

Now my dad had never met a priest before and he didn't know what you're supposed to say to a priest, nor—most importantly—what you're not supposed to say.

I'd been living in Ireland a couple of years by that stage and I'd learned that priests were treated differently to other people (much like the Queen, Dolly Parton, and that fellow who stands on your street corner claiming the world is going to end). I'd learned that there were special 'priest rules'; rules that were unspoken but known by everyone, or at least everyone who lived there. I knew a few of the rules, however, my dad knew none. I'm not sure how it happened but he'd ended up sitting next to the priest.

The official wedding stuff had just finished, and I watched Dad turn to the priest.

He said, "What's it like living with all those nuns then?"

I think I flinched.

To be fair, that is an interesting question especially if you don't know the answer, but it was definitely not the sort of thing you're supposed to ask a priest.

The table suddenly went silent. Everyone had heard the question and no matter whether they knew the official answer or not (which FYI is that the priests and nuns don't normally live together), they were all desperately keen to hear the answer.

The priest raised one eyebrow, paused to think before answering, and then smiled.

"It's like being nibbled to death by ducklings."

And everyone else at the table, including my dad, smiled because they all knew exactly what he meant.

CHAPTER 2

CHURCHILL

The 'Agadir crisis' kicked off when, in retaliation for France moving 20,000 troops into Morocco, the German leader, Kaiser Wilhelm, thumbed his nose (geopolitically speaking) at France. First, he sent a gunboat then, a few days later, a larger warship to sit menacingly in Agadir's port.

I'd never heard of this crisis until one day I was out on a bike ride half-heartedly listening to the BBC's More or Less podcast. My ears perked up because the host had just mentioned this place called Agadir and I had one of those funny moments when you know there's something significant about a word, but you can't quite put your finger on it.

I was intrigued, so I gave the podcast my full attention while I let the librarian who lives in the back of my brain get to work, chugging away in the background searching my memories for the word Agadir.

The host then mentioned something I did not expect.

He said that World War One *almost* started there, in Agadir, in 1911.

"That's odd," I muttered to myself. I was sure that

World War One started when an Austrian general got assassinated.

So, I kept listening while my brain kept churning through my memories.

The host explained that the French and British leaders —who'd been busy carving up Africa for themselves—interpreted Germany's move as a blatant challenge to their global positions, which it was. The British leaders believed the Germans were going to turn Agadir into their Atlantic naval base which would weaken them, so they sent one of their own battleships to Morocco, just in case war broke out.

This was a colonial turf war, but no one wanted a real war, so Europe's leaders met, hoping to prevent war. The rest of the world watched and waited anxiously. The negotiations were intense but fruitful, and everyone avoided war, temporarily. But everyone of importance, including Winston Churchill and the British Prime Minister, knew that *war was inevitable.*

Shortly afterwards, the British PM appointed Churchill —a young man, still in his thirties—to the role of First Lord of the Admiralty and instructed him to prepare the British navy to win a war against Germany.

The podcast's host, the economist Tim Harford, went on to explain how Churchill immediately found himself having to make a particularly difficult choice, a dilemma:

- **Should Britain's navy (a) stick with coal-powered ships or (b) switch to the new, more powerful oil-powered ships?**

If you're like me, sitting here with the wisdom that comes with over a century's worth of hindsight, the obvious answer was to switch to oil-powered ships. Oil packs in a lot more energy compared to coal. The ships are faster and smaller. They can travel further, and they can stay out at sea longer. So, obviously: oil is the answer.

But it wasn't as simple as that. If it was that simple, he would have just made the decision, and got on with building the new ships.

But something held him back. What was it?

My Mission: Build A Strong Navy that can win a war against Germany.

THE PROBLEM with oil-powered ships is that the oil came from thousands of miles away in Iran (then called Persia) by sea, either through the Suez Canal or via Cape of Good Hope near the southern tip of Africa, so it was neither secure nor reliable. Oil-powered ships would be more powerful, but without a reliable and secure fuel supply, they'd end up stuck in port, or worse, floating at sea like sitting ducks. Britain would almost certainly lose the coming war.

So, they had to stick with coal-powered warships, right? Wrong.

Yes, coal was a reliable fuel source, but the German navy was almost certainly switching to oil. They were already building oil cruise ships, and their oil supply would travel over land from the middle east to Germany. For Britain to stick with coal power, as the movie line goes, would be like 'bringing a knife to a gunfight.'

So, both options had a lot going for them, but neither was good. Churchill could flip a coin and whatever way it landed; Britain was likely to lose the war.

———

THIS TYPE OF SITUATION—WHERE **you must make a seemingly impossible choice between two good (or bad) alternatives—is called a 'dilemma.'**

CHAPTER 3

DUCKLINGS AND DILEMMAS

Whenever I work with someone new, I almost always start out by telling them the little story about my dad, the Priest, and the Killer Ducklings. And then, after they've politely chuckled, they look at me quizzically, as if they're wondering if I offer refunds.

So, I ask them if it ever feels like *they* are being nibbled to death by ducklings.

And they all do.

They know this is a metaphor, of course, and that the ducklings represent the problems, distractions, annoyances, worries, concerns, and little persnickety details that take up too much space in their brains. They're little things, the ducklings, and they're fluffy and cute. None of their little nips actually hurt, but they're annoying, and they cause us to spend too much of our precious energy to gently—but constantly—swat them away.

Ducklings suck the oxygen out of the room.

They rob us of the energy and time we should be devoting to thinking about and doing the bigger and more important things.

They distract us away from the important towards the urgent and that slowly kills us.

Just like real ducklings, these imaginary ducklings grow bigger and bigger over time. The bigger they get the more their nips hurt, and they keep pooping all over the place and you waste even more of your precious time cleaning it up.

Most folk waste a lot of their time dealing with killer ducklings—the symptoms.

Wise people reclaim that wasted time by finding the root cause of all those distractions.

———

HERE'S MY CLAIM: **unresolved dilemmas are the #1 cause of killer ducklings.**

CHAPTER 4

TAKING SIDES

So there Churchill is, faced with his unresolved dilemma.

Does he stick with coal, and lose the war? Or does he convert to oil, and lose the war?

When faced with dilemmas like this, most of us tend to pick one position (often based on an emotional reaction or some other bias), and then we vigorously argue for our position over the other.

In other words, we take sides.

This side-taking creates a lot of ducklings.

Roll your mind back to 1911. Churchill is new in his job and everyone knows he is faced with this difficult, seemingly impossible decision.

Can you imagine a delegation that includes some of the navy's most forward-thinking and best engineers and officers, assembling in Churchill's Whitehall offices, arguing vigorously in favor of oil?

- "Ignore the Luddites and dinosaurs, this war will be won on the high seas! How can we

possibly win when our enemy's navy is more powerful, more agile than ours?"
- "We must at least match Germany's warships, otherwise we will be defeated."
- "All we need to do is secure the fuel supply. Germany's done it, so can we!"

Obviously, from their point of view, oil was the very best choice.

Can you also imagine, later that day Churchill meets with another delegation—also made up of some of his best officers and engineers—and they're warning him to ignore the gadget freaks and early adopters, and arguing the virtues of coal-powered ships?

- "What use are more powerful ships if they run out of fuel?"
- "We can't safely ship troops and supplies if our warships are stuck in port and unable to protect our transport ships."
- "We must stick with what we know—that's always been our strength."

For them, coal was the only logical choice.

To complicate matters, picture much later that same evening, a dark, luxurious men's club, filled with cigar smoke, where a coalition of politicians and coal-mine owners are trying to convince Churchill over port and brandy that coal is the only safe option—even though everyone in the room knows this is an argument about political power and coal revenues, not war.

Of course, these meetings weren't one-offs—they kept repeating, day after day. Sometimes with the same people, sometimes with others, each of them repeating the same arguments but with minor variations. No doubt, as the arguments went on and on, they got more and more detailed, and over time, became nasty and personal.

So, there's Churchill, stuck in the middle. He can't take sides because as far as he's concerned his advisors are already all on the same side, even if they don't always act like it. He knows the true enemy is, literally, across the sea in Germany, building warships.

He also knows that to win the impending war, he needs to stop listening to the arguments going on around him, and solve the problem in a different way, a wiser way.

He must treat the **dilemma as the enemy**.

But how did he do that?

He didn't choose one side over the other.

He created a third solution that both sides agreed on.

CHAPTER 5

PROBLEM-PINBALL

Have you ever played Problem-Pinball?
You're human so I bet you have.

Problem-Pinball is nature's way of telling us that we have a serious problem, and we need to fix it.

It is much like normal pinball, except it's played with thoughts and worries (aka killer ducklings) rather than shiny balls, and they bounce around inside your head (usually at 3 A.M) rather than inside a pinball machine.

It's free, in the sense that you can play it over and over and over, but you don't have to hand over money to play it. It is very costly though. The game consumes a lot of your time, takes up a lot of space in your brain, and—since it's a vicious circle—it never achieves anything.

I'm sure you've played it many, many times over the years. I have.

But here's the thing: you can't play Problem-Pinball unless you have an important unresolved dilemma.

When you solve a seemingly impossible dilemma, the pinballs stop, and the ducklings disappear.

CHAPTER 6

CHURCHILL-PINBALL

C hurchill had a thicker skin than most, but I bet he lay awake at night playing Problem-Pinball. Let me show you how his games would have played out. Follow along with this diagram.

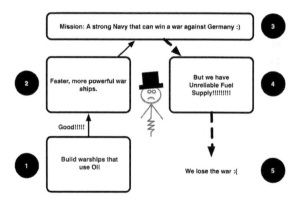

It's 3 A.M., Churchill wakes up, his mind turning over

and over because he's worried (because he's facing an urgent, important unresolved dilemma):

1. His mind kicks off the game by firing off the ball on the left-hand side of the dilemma—"We build oil-powered warships."
2. He watches in his mind's eye as the ball flies up directly to the benefits of that option—"We have fast, powerful ships!"
3. He keeps watching as it flies up the table to the mission—"We win the war! Yay!" He smiles to himself.
4. But then he frowns as inside his head he watches the ball fall back down into this option's big negative outcome—"Our ships run out of fuel."
5. He grumbles to himself as the ball falls down and then off the table because he's lost the game —"We lose the war."

If he was born in a different era, his brain might well have made that awful wah-wah-wah sound real games make to indicate that you've lost a ball or a life.

So, it is 3 A.M. in the morning and his mind is whirring in that discombobulating way it does at that time of day— when you're half-asleep, half-awake—when his mind suddenly remembers something, "Hang on, our ships wouldn't run out of fuel if we stick with coal!"

Which, of course, is the other option.

So, his brain automatically fires off the ball on the right-hand side of the dilemma:

1. If "We stick with warships that use coal."

2. The benefit: "We will have a reliable fuel supply."
3. The mission: "We will win the war" . . .
4. But negative outcome: "The enemy will have more powerful ships than us."
5. And "We lose the war."

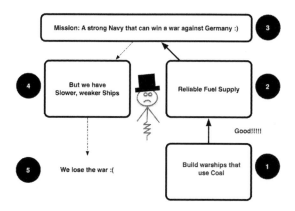

Cue the depressing 'you lose' wah-wah-wah sound.

But then his brain perks up and remembers that what we really needed all along is powerful ships . . . which is what you'd get if you chose the oil option . . . and . . . the game starts all over again.

Rather than realizing he can't win this game and falling back to sleep, he fruitlessly repeats the two pinball scenarios over and over in his head until he either eventually falls back to sleep, or gives up and gets out of bed, tired and grumpy, already feeling defeated, and it's not even 5 A.M. yet.

Problem-Pinball is a vicious cycle. It gets kicked off

whenever you have an unresolved, urgent dilemma. You play it at work during the day, and inside your head in the middle of the night. The longer the unresolved dilemma exists, the more ducklings are created, and the bigger they grow. Before you know it, you're knee-deep in duck poop with no shovel, and no time to tackle the real problem.

When you repeatedly wake up at 3 A.M. to play pinball, that's your mind telling you that you are trapped inside a dilemma and you have to do something about it, something different.

You need a trick; you need to think outside the box—because the standard approach of taking sides doesn't work.

CHAPTER 7

CHURCHILL'S CLOUD

There are actually two tricks to solving these seemingly unsolvable dilemmas.

Let me show you.

The first trick is to make the dilemmas visible by untangling the arguments and stripping them down to their bare essentials.

Churchill is sick of playing Problem-Pinball, so he sits down and asks himself:

What's my mission, Winston?
To prepare the navy to win a war.

What are the two conflicting alternatives?
Build oil-powered ships, or build coal-powered ships.

What are the benefits of both?
Oil-powered ships are *faster and more powerful.*
Coal-powered ships *have a safe and reliable fuel supply.*

Maybe he then draws out a little 5-box diagram (it's called a "cloud" and, yes, I know, it looks an awful lot like a combination of the two Problem-Pinball diagrams from earlier).

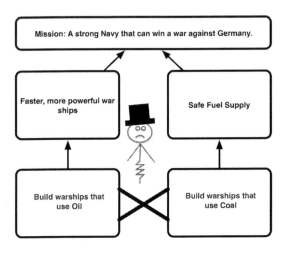

Read through that. It should sum up everything we have discussed so far, and also place structure around the arguments.

All unresolved dilemmas fit inside this same 5-box structure.

There's an old saying that *if you can't measure something, you can't manage it.* When we are solving problems a more useful saying is *if you can't see something, you can't fix it.* The cloud diagram helps you see the dilemma.

And, if you'll forgive me a dad-joke: it helps you get your ducklings in a row.

With the dilemma stripped naked and on display in front of us, we're ready to apply the second trick.

The second trick is to identify the benefits of each competing alternative, then figure out how to get both.

Imagine Churchill staring at the two boxes in the middle row of the diagram—the benefits.

He mutters, "I must invent a solution that gives me both benefits."

I can see him nodding to himself.

He says, "It doesn't matter what fuel the warships use so long as they are **both** *fast and powerful* **and** *have a safe fuel supply.*"

He considers each option, one at a time.

He asks, "How can I have coal-powered ships . . . that are also fast and powerful?"

He shakes his head. "My engineers are working on that, but I don't hold out much hope."

He grimaces, then asks a different question. "What would I have to do for my oil-powered ships . . . to also have a safe fuel supply?"

He mulls.

"I'd need to ensure the safety of fuel supply ships on their journey from Persia to England."

He thinks a little, nods, then mumbles, "I can find a way to do that."

He frowns. "But will that be enough?"

He shakes his head. "No, it won't. Even if the trip is 100% safe, the fundamental problem is that we do not own the oil company—foreign interests do—and when war breaks out, they can sell their oil to whomever they want to. We could end up in a bidding war against the Germans, and we can't guarantee that we'd win."

Maybe at that moment, he felt the flicker of a lightbulb coming to life inside his head.

Maybe he smiled because he knew that all he had to do was wait for the idea to fully form.

And it did.

Several months later the British government purchased a 51 percent share in the Anglo-Persian Oil Company—the same company that would become British Petroleum—BP.

Owning the oil supply was the 'tent pole' tactic that his entire strategy was built around, but there was more work after that of course:

- His shipyards started building new oil-powered warships.
- His staff got to work figuring out military and diplomatic solutions that would secure the production and transportation of oil.
- He also, rather cleverly, decided to limit the amount of oil his navy needed, by only converting the warships to oil and leaving the other ships running on coal.

And while all that was going on, he continued negotiating with his German counterparts, hoping to slow down ship production on both sides, and perhaps prevent a war.

This was all hard work, and no doubt birthed a whole flock of new ducklings, but the old ducklings disappeared in a puff of imaginary yellow feathers the moment he decided to buy the oil company.

Let's take one last look at the cloud diagram as it stands after Britain bought the oil company.

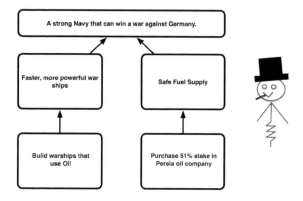

Notice how the two options do not conflict?

Churchill's navy got the *best of both worlds* **and his powerful, reliable ships were instrumental in winning World War One.**

PART 2

THE CLOUD

CHAPTER 8

ELI GOLDRATT

The diagram we used to draw out Churchill's dilemma is formally called an 'evaporating cloud,' but I just call it a 'cloud.'

It's the invention of my hero Eli Goldratt, author of *The Goal*, and father of the Theory of Constraints. He introduced the evaporating cloud to the world in his business novel, *It's Not Luck*. It is his easiest and most powerful invention.

The cloud has two parts:

1. A diagram that describes a dilemma, and
2. A process for filling out the diagram then using it to resolve the dilemma.

Before I walk you through the process, let me show you some filled-out clouds. You should understand them easily enough. It's a good idea to read them twice—first from the bottom up, then from the top down. Please, take your time and become familiar with the shape of the cloud.

Here's a cloud you may have faced sometime in your life:

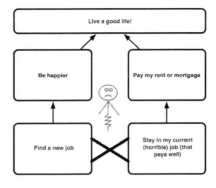

Here's another one you might be considering right now:

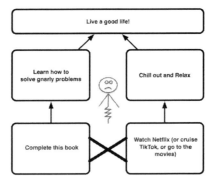

Here's a cloud that tormented almost every student in a course I taught on a business school grad program[1]:

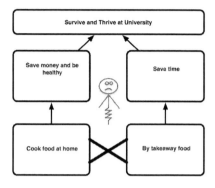

Here's a slightly gnarlier cloud (and slightly different looking) from my book, *Rolling Rocks Downhill*:

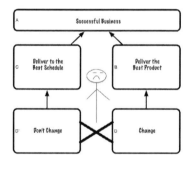

I'M NOT sure whether the old management cliché that says you can't manage what you can't measure is true or not, but I'm convinced that you can't solve what you can't see.

The cloud helps you see the dilemma so that you can solve it.

Dilemmas are often very good at hiding. Before you draw the diagram, you're faced with what my dad used to call 'a dog's breakfast'—it's an expression that came from a time when dogs ate a hodgepodge of yesterday's scraps and leftovers for their breakfast, rather than mass-produced and neatly packaged tinned and bagged food.

After you've drawn the diagram, the dilemma looks tidier and structured, more like a puzzle.

It helps that all dilemmas share the same structure:

- Top Row = The mission.
- Middle Row = The 2 benefits.
- Bottom row = The 2 conflicting options.

CHAPTER 9

BOB THE STICK FIGURE

D id you notice the odd-looking stick figure in the middle of each cloud?

His name is CorkScrew BoB.

He's our guide.

This is what he looks like from close up:

I think of BoB as a cross between Yoda and Microsoft Clippy, though he's not nearly as irritating as either.

If you're too young to understand those references, then . . . I've been told that you might like to think of BoB as a cross between Taylor Swift and Siri.

BoB started life as a memory trick—a mnemonic—that I

invented on the spot many years ago when my friend Graeme and I were out on a long drive through the Highlands of Scotland, trying to tackle a few gnarly problems going on in his work life.

We needed to draw a couple of clouds, but we couldn't because we were driving and didn't have a pen or paper.

"Why don't we stop at a pub?" he said with considerable enthusiasm. "We could draw the clouds on the back of beer mats or on napkins."

Graeme likes pubs and stopping at a pub is one of his favorite problem-solving techniques, but I don't and since I was driving, I kept going and suggested that instead of using a beer mat, we could just pick 5 body parts—2 hands, 2 shoulders and 1 head—to represent the boxes.

"Like Sherlock Holmes remembered things in his memory palace?" he asked.

"Yeah."

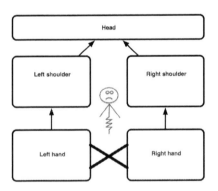

So that's what we did, and as it turned out, the body parts we chose were—thankfully—not only safe for work but also, coincidentally, related to the parts of the cloud they represent.

Working from the bottom two boxes up:

The bottom boxes are the HANDS.

- They're our two conflicting alternatives.
- They're actions.
- You already use this kind of language to describe a conflict—"Well, on the one HAND, I could do X, but on the other HAND, I could do Y."

The middle two boxes are the SHOULDERS.

- They're what you get out of doing the stuff on the hand below them—the benefits.
- Think of them as the 'weights on your SHOULDERS'—the things you worry about, especially when you don't have them.
- Think of Atlas, the poor Greek god who had to carry the world around on his shoulders, but imagine he had to carry two different worlds, one on each shoulder.

The top box is the HEAD.

- Think of this box as your mission or purpose.
- If you're in an argument with someone else or trying to work with two parties who are arguing, then think of this box as the mutual purpose they share that keeps them working on the problem.
- I don't always fill out this box.

This body-part approach worked really well with Graeme and before long, whenever I explained how to draw a cloud, I drew the stick figure first and then built the boxes up around it.

I dunno why I first called the little stick figure Bob. It was a random choice, I think. I tend to refer to him as "him" though, for all I know, she could just as easily be "her."

Many years passed before Bob became CorkScrew BoB. BoB has two capitalized 'B's because his or her name has become an acronym. I'll tell you more about that later.

CHAPTER 10

TWO FORMATS

I f you're already familiar with Eli Goldratt's original format, you'll recognize that I've turned his diagram 90 degrees clockwise, and added in the stick figure like this:

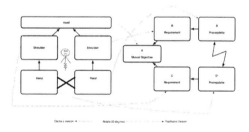

The two formats are interchangeable, but many people tell me they find my vertical layout easier to work with.

As you will see later, there are many ways to draw, type or write a cloud.

PART 3

LET'S DRAW A CLOUD

CHAPTER 11

INTRODUCING GEORGIE

Georgie is a rescue dog—she was found abandoned on the side of the road along with her 5 brothers, and now lives with us.

It was love at first bite—tiny playful puppy bites, of course, not distracting duckling nips— and we've been best friends ever since. When we first got her, I went all glassy-eyed for a moment and pictured a future  where she and I traveled the world together solving crimes, much like Scooby-Doo did with his friends—except we'd stay in nice hotels and as part of the adoption process we'd change her name to Dogatha Christie. That hasn't happened yet, but most weekends, my wife, kids and I do take Georgie to one of our local beaches, either for a walk, a swim, or to chase pinecones.

The only thing Georgie loves as much as chasing pinecones is eating food.

A few weeks ago, Georgie got herself in a bit of a bind, that lasted about half a second.

Here's what happened.

- We arrived at the beach, parked, got out of our car, then released Georgie.
- Then, without checking to see what my wife was doing, I marched off in one direction, found a pinecone, picked it up, then shouted "Georgie, Georgie, Georgie."
- What I hadn't realized is that as I walked in one direction, my wife strode off in the exact opposite direction, pulled some treats from her food stash, turned to face Georgie and shouted out "Georgie, Georgie, Georgie."

Georgie was torn. She was conflicted. She was, for a brief moment, stuck inside a dilemma. She was pulled—literally—in two opposite directions.

I watched as her head spun from me to my wife and back to me again.

I could see what she was thinking:

- Should she run to me . . . to the pinecone?
- Should she run to my wife . . . to the food?

She couldn't do both.

CHAPTER 12

START WITH A BLANK CLOUD

L et's use this very simple (but true) example to learn the steps to draw out a cloud.

My imaginary friend CorkScrew Bob will help.

He starts by drawing out a blank 'cloud' diagram.

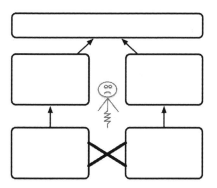

BoB asks Georgie to describe the dilemma.

She says that she is clearly torn between two very appealing options.

- **On the one paw**, I could chase the pinecone.
- **On the other paw**, I could run to the food.

BoB fills out the bottom row of the cloud—the two hands/paws.

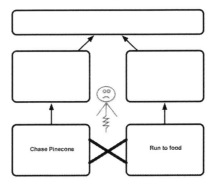

Pretty simple, right?

1. You start with two *conflicting* options.
2. You write them in the two hand boxes.
3. You double-check that they do indeed conflict—that they are mutually exclusive.

BoB reminds Georgie that the shoulders are:

- *The benefits* she'd get from choosing each alternative, or to put that another way,
- *What she'd miss out on* if she chose the other option.

BoB starts with the left shoulder.

What do you get out of chasing the pinecone, Georgie?

Georgie says, "I chase the pine cone for fun!"

BoB writes that in the left-hand shoulder box: "Have Fun."

He switches to the right-hand shoulder and asks, "What do you get out of running toward the food?"

Georgie frowns as if that's a stupid question, "I get fed, of course."

BoB pops those words on the diagram.

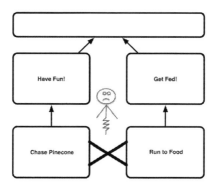

BoB pauses a moment to sanity check what he's written so far.

He uses a simple template: "In order to SHOULDER we must HAND."

He says:

- "In order to HAVE FUN you must CHASE PINECONE," and
- "In order to GET FOOD, you must RUN TO FOOD."

Georgie tilts her head from side to side, then nods, "That's it."

CHAPTER 13

THE HEAD

B oB asks Georgie what her mission is.

She says, "To have fun and get fed!"

BoB says, "No . . . The mission is something bigger than that—it's not just the sum of the two shoulders."

Georgie says, "Oh . . ."

BoB explains that you can think of the top box—the HEAD—as your mission or purpose but warns Georgie to not overthink things.

He said, "There's no need to book into an off-site location, hire an expensive facilitator, and spend two days writing a mission statement."

Georgie nods.

BoB adds, "If you were managing a project, your mission is probably to deliver a project with good outcomes, which you could shorten to 'successful project.' If you're running a small business, your mission is probably to have a profitable, sustainable business. If you're writing a book, your mission might be to 'publish a book I'm proud of' or 'publish a book that makes money.'"

Georgie says, "Look, I just wanna chase the pinecone and get fed."

BoB shrugs, then says, "Since this is a family trip to the beach, would you be happy with 'everyone has a great trip to the beach?'"

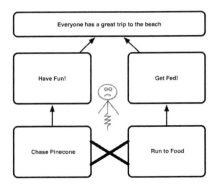

Georgie says, 'I just want to be a good dog."
BoB writes that at the top.

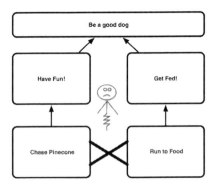

CHAPTER 14

CREATE NEW OPTIONS

This imagined conversation between BoB and Georgie took less than half a second since, in the real world, no one would bother drawing a cloud for something so easily resolved.

That's because it's a really easy dilemma to solve.

Georgie didn't just stand there with her head spinning from side to side, overwhelmed by choice and paralyzed into inaction. She didn't suddenly start chasing ducklings (as much as she'd love to) because—guess what?—the ducklings did not have time to appear.

Instead, she ran to the food first, and then having satisfied her need to get fed, she turned and ran to me so that she could have fun chasing the pinecone.

Here's the new version of our cloud:

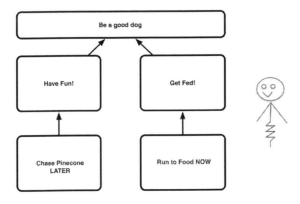

Notice that BoB the stick figure is now smiling and the cross has gone.

Take a look at the wording of the two boxes.

The two options are no longer mutually exclusive.

And all it took was a change in wording: adding the word 'LATER' to one option, and the word 'NOW' to the other.

That, by the way, is the essence of what we're doing here:

- We start with two conflicting options, and,
- We end with options that don't conflict.

Georgie got the best of both worlds, by editing a few words on an imaginary diagram.

CHAPTER 15

ACRONYM

CorkScrew BoB's name is an acronym that stands for 'Best of Both.'

When you're stuck, you should ask yourself, "What would BoB do?"

BoB would:

- Find the two conflicting options,
- Figure out the benefits of both,
- Come up with new options that get both benefits and, therefore, the **best of both** worlds.

PART 4

EVERY DAY INTEGRATIVE THINKING

CHAPTER 16

ROGER L. MARTIN -
INTEGRATIVE THINKING

R oger L. Martin is one of the world's greatest management thinkers and author of the brilliantly named books, *The Opposable Mind* and *Creating Great Choices*, amongst others. A few years ago, he was voted by one management website as the #1 Management Thinker in the world. He's clever and also a nice fellow.

In the 2000s, he studied a bunch of highly successful leaders.

He was trying to find out what they had in common, and what distinguished them from everyone else.

He made a startling discovery.

He discovered that although the leaders "shared little by way of context or background, they all used *integrative thinking* to solve their toughest problems" and that *integrative thinking* is the ONE THING that sets highly successful leaders apart from the masses.

Integrative Thinking?

Sounds like powerful stuff!

What is it?

He said that all of these leaders had "the predisposition and the capability to hold two diametrically opposing ideas in their heads. And then, without panicking or simply settling for one alternative or the other, they're able to produce a synthesis that is superior to either opposing idea."

That's a hefty sentence so let me unpack.

Great leaders:

- Take two conflicting ("diametrically opposed") ideas.
- They don't panic or takes sides.
- Instead, they hold both ideas in their head, then
- They create (synthesize) new, better ideas.

That's exactly how we solve gnarly problems using clouds.

We all already do integrative thinking. We do it intuitively when faced with easy to solve dilemmas. Great leaders use it when facing harder problems. That's one of the skills that makes them great.

Eli Goldratt was one of those great leaders and he knew he thought differently. But he didn't know *how* he thought differently, and that bugged him, so he sat down and figured that out. The result was his cloud diagram and process.

You're learning a simpler and easier version of his process here.

You are learning: *Integrative Thinking Using Clouds*.

Which is a dreadful acronym—*ITUC*.

Instead, I call it *Every Day Integrative Thinking*, or *EDIT*.

CHAPTER 17

EDIT AND EDITING

The IT bit of EDIT stands for Integrative Thinking (obviously).

The ED bit of EDIT stands for 'Every Day' because you'll use it every day, and 'EveryDay' because I'm assuming that you're an everyday sort of person.

I chose the acronym very carefully.

When you use the EDIT process you are working with words.

You're writing then rewriting words—i.e., editing them.

When you draw out a cloud you start by pulling words out of your head. You write the words down, rewrite them, read them out loud, and rewrite them again, and maybe again. Edit, edit, edit.

Once you've written your cloud, you start to edit it again but you're no longer describing the conflict, you're trying to get rid of it—to write it out of history, so to speak. You'll add words to one text box. You'll cross out words in another. You'll add new options (hands). You'll keep writing, and rewriting, until you've written yourself out of the dilemma.

With each cloud, you're editing your present and rewriting yourself into a new future.

Let me show you two more clouds.

One from Georgie. One from Winston.

I'll then compare and contrast them on a fancy 2x2 matrix.

PART 5

DIFFICULT CLOUDS VS. IMPORTANT CLOUDS

CHAPTER 18

BATH TIME

T his cloud may seem trivial, perhaps even silly:

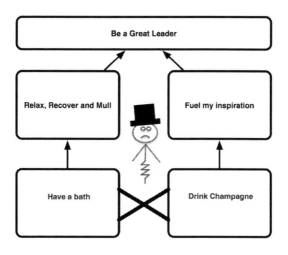

Here are two things I know about Churchill:

1. He liked baths and did a lot of his best thinking while in the bath.
2. He liked drinking.

He is reputed to have drunk over 40,000 bottles of Champagne.

He once said, "I've gotten more out of alcohol than alcohol has taken out of me."

Perhaps he was an alcoholic who didn't function so well when he was sober; perhaps alcohol was like a fuel that helped him think better.

Who knows?

Whatever the answer, I imagine that many of his most momentous decisions were made either in the bath or while 'inspired' by alcohol.

So, why not combine the two?

Get the best of both worlds?

Drink champagne in the bath.

What was stopping him?

Nothing other than convention.

And Churchill didn't really care for convention.

CHAPTER 19

BAD DOG?

H ere's another cloud.

Occasionally Georgie raids the rubbish bin in our kitchen.

I know that she knows that she's not meant to do it because she never does it when we are there in the kitchen.

And when we catch her, she looks guilty.

And then she gets growled at.

But, being a clever dog, she ignores my threats to return her to the rescue center and raids the bin whenever she can. Which was, until recently, most days.

Her cloud looks something like this.

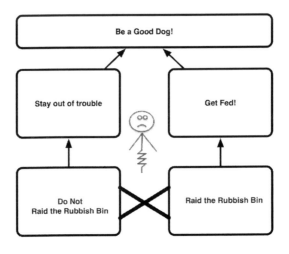

My wife and I resolved this dilemma a few weeks ago by moving the bin into the pantry, which she couldn't get into. And then, after I drew out this cloud on Georgie's behalf, I went and bought a dog-proof kitchen bin for $40. And then, two days later we discovered that, despite the clear labeling on the new bin saying it is "Dog Proof," it wasn't dog proof.

We're still working on this cloud.

CHAPTER 20

THE CLOUD 2X2

L et's contrast Georgie's two clouds and Churchill's two clouds, using a 2x2 diagram with these 2 axes: Importance and Difficulty.

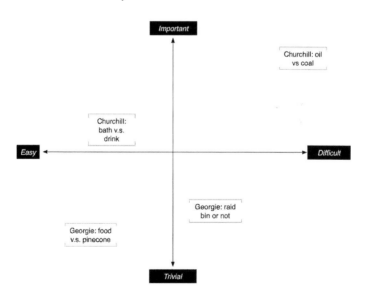

You might place them differently. That's okay.
Here's what I'd like you to notice:

- Some clouds are easier to solve than others;
- Some clouds are more important than others.
- The easier clouds get solved quickly and often disappear immediately without you ever noticing them.
- Harder clouds hang around.

No matter who you are or what you do, you already instinctively solve dilemmas using Integrative Thinking every day. Yay, you!

They are the (so-called) "easy" dilemmas on the left side of the 2x2 diagram.

The EDIT process helps you tackle dilemmas that currently sit in on the right of the diagram in your "too hard basket."

PART 6

FRIENDS

CHAPTER 21

THE LIBRARIAN

I have a theory that there's a little librarian living in the back of my brain (and everyone else's brains) who fetches memories for me.

If the memory is easy to find, the *Librarian* finds it and returns it quickly, if not instantly.

On the other hand, if the memory had long ago been bubble-wrapped, put in a box, then stored somewhere along with millions of other memories deep down inside the dark basement that sits at the back of your brain . . . the *Librarian* has some serious digging to do, so it takes a lot longer.

It took my *Librarian* a day and a half to remember where I'd heard the word 'Agadir' before.

My wife and I spent a week in Agadir on a sun-filled vacation shortly after we got married. They had nice olives. I got food poisoning. I don't know if the two were related. No one ever mentioned that WW1 almost started there.

When I told my wife this, she told me she could've told me that if I'd asked her.

The librarian has 3 friends. They work together to solve problems.

I'll introduce them to you shortly.

But, before I introduce you to them, I need to reacquaint you with 5 friends from the 1990s.

CHAPTER 22

FRIENDS 1

I bet you've seen or watched the TV show 'Friends'. I watched it 25 years ago. My daughters watch it (and re-watch it) nowadays.

It's a love story hidden inside a situation comedy.

You probably remember the episode called 'The One with the List.'

It could have been 'The One with the Mocolate' or 'The One with the Sad U2 Song at the End.'

It was episode 8 in series 2.

Episode 7 had ended on a cliff-hanger:

Ross and Rachel had—finally—kissed.

Kissed!

Finally!

This kiss was good news for everyone watching the show because deep down we all knew that Ross and Rachel belonged together, forever.

The only people who didn't know that were Ross and Rachel.

Oh, and Julie.

Julie was Ross's girlfriend.

THREE MINUTES INTO THE EPISODE, Ross is sitting in The Central Perk—the coffee shop with the huge couch —and he looks miserable.

He sounds miserable too.

"What the hell am I doing?" he says. "Here I am with Julie, this incredible, great woman who I care about and who cares about me and I'm like, am I just going to throw all of that away?"

Monica, his sister says, "But you're talking about Rachel."

Ross nods, thoughtfully, then looks even glummer. "I've been dreaming about Rachel for 10 years."

He then holds his left hand out in front of him, Cork-Screw BoB-style, and says, "Me and Julie."

Then, as if weighing up his two options on a set of scales, he lowers his left hand and raises his right. "Me and Rachel."

He repeats the motion.

On the one hand: "Me and Julie."

On the other hand: "Me and Rachel."

Ross is, as the saying goes, stuck between a rock and a hard place.

This type of situation, as you know, is called a dilemma.

———

ROSS'S cloud mighta looked something like this:

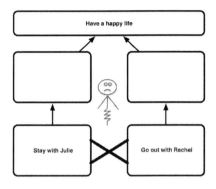

The two hands are clear.

They usually are.

The shoulders, on the other hand, are murkier.

CHAPTER 23

UPTHINKING

I call the process of figuring out what words sit on CorkScrew BoB's shoulders *UpThinking*.

It's a word I made up.

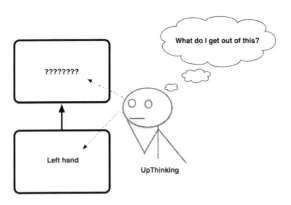

Imagine BoB standing there looking at one of the hand boxes. He looks *UP* to the shoulder box directly above the hand box and *THINKS* up answers to the question, 'What do I get out of this?'

He *UpThinks*.

And then, once the benefits sitting on BoB's shoulders are clear, he can *Think Up* new options.

There are three ways to do *UpThinking*

Let's look at the first two ways - they're easy.

———

THE FIRST QUESTION TO ask is always:

- *'What do I get out of doing this alternative?'*

Like this:

What do we get out of switching to oil-powered ships?
Power and speed.

Let's try it with Ross's dilemma.

What does Ross get out of staying with Julie?
Ummm . . . he gets to stay with Julie.

That doesn't add any new useful information, so let's ask the same question but in a different way.

———

OFTENTIMES, rather than asking what you get out of choosing an option, you get richer answers by asking what you lose by choosing the alternative option:

- *'What do I lose by choosing the other alternative?'*

or

- *'What would I jeopardize if I chose the other alternative?'*

Like this:

What's jeopardized by switching to oil?
Our ships are highly likely to run out of fuel.

Let's try this with Ross's dilemma.

What does Ross lose by choosing to go out with Rachel?

He loses Julie.

That doesn't add any new information either. We will need to use the third type of *UpThinking*.

Before I show you how that works, let me introduce the *Librarian's other friends*.

CHAPTER 24

THE PATTERN MAKER, THE
EDITOR AND THE WHY FINDER

T*he Librarian*'s three friends are:

- The *Pattern Maker, who is constantly on the lookout for fluffy clouds floating in the sky that look like Richard Nixon, puns, and other patterns.*
- The *Editor*, who likes simplifying and cleaning things up.
- The *Why Finder, who* is really good at coming up with plausible-sounding explanations.

The *Librarian* and her three imaginary friends work very well together when you're trying to draw thoughts out from the deep, dark depths of your brain and transform them into explicit clear thoughts.

They all have their faults,[1] and I specifically need to point out that the *Why Finder* is chronically lazy.

Ask your *Why Finder* a question and you will almost always get a plausible explanation. It'll not necessarily be the best or most useful explanation. It may not even be true.

The lazy *Why Finder* favors the answers that are easiest to retrieve.

Let me show you what I mean.

1. When I first heard about Churchill's Navy dilemma, my *Why Finder* told me Churchill wanted to stick with coal because he was friends with the coal mine owners and was trying to protect his political position and their revenues.
2. When I thought 'surely there's more to it than that?' my *Why Finder* told me you'd stick with coal because the trip from Persia to England was long, insecure, and dangerous.
3. When I learned that Churchill bought a majority stake in the Persian oil company, my *Why Finder* said that was because a foreign company didn't have to sell their product to Churchill's Navy.

To make the most of your *Why Finder*, you need to keep asking 'Why,' 'Why,' 'Why?' until you are happy that you know what's going on.

Don't just take their first answer.

Make them work.

Make them make 2 lists: reasons for and reasons against.

Pros and cons, in other words.

CHAPTER 25

FRIENDS 2

Recognizing he has a dilemma, Ross asks his male friends, Joey and Chandler, for help.

Joey makes a suggestion that might work in the short term, but definitely would not work in the long term. Ross dismisses it.

Chandler—who'd just got a new work laptop (with 12 Megabytes of RAM and a 500 Megabyte hard disk, no less!) —offers, instead, to help Ross write out a pros and cons list for each woman using the computer's built-in spreadsheet capabilities.

A pros and cons list.[1]

He's enlisting help from Ross's *Why Finder*, seeking a brain dump of answers to these 4 questions:

Rachel Pros – What are the benefits of going out with Rachel?
Rachel Cons – What are the negatives of going out with Rachel?
Julie Pros – What are the benefits of staying with Julie?

Julie Cons – What are the negatives of staying with Julie?

Simple, right?

Chandler and Ross start listing out the cons for Rachel. Ross says Rachel is:

- "spoiled,"
- "ditzy,"
- "too into her looks" and
- "just a waitress."

And then, if those weren't enough, he adds that:

- "she has chubby ankles."

Ouch.

But then when he tries to list out cons for Julie he is stumped.

He can't think of a single negative thing to say about her.

Awww.

It's like she is perfect.

But, if she's perfect, why doesn't he just stick with her? Why can't he just forget about Rachel and live happily ever after with Julie?

Why *Finder*, Why?

Ross goes quiet.

He's thinking.

His *Why Finder* and *Pattern Maker* are busy working together to figure out what's going on inside his head.

Suddenly, Ross shakes his head and blurts out, "She's not Rachel."

CHAPTER 26

UPTHINKING – PROS AND CONS QUESTIONS

W hen I make my pros and cons lists, I go into bullet-point mode on my PC, tablet or phone and just start typing. I brain dump the pros and cons for both options without trying to get them perfect, and I keep going until I run out of oomph. I let my *Why Finder* and *Pattern Maker* bounce thoughts off each other, while my fingertips do the typing. I do not ever let my *Editor* help me out—I'm seeking speed and quantity, not spelling and grammatical perfection.

You can see my version of what Churchill's 4 lists might have looked like by following this footnote. [1]

Once I've done my brain dump I'll often get up and walk around a bit, but then I come back to the 4 lists and I come up with short, pithy summary sentences for both shoulders. That's when the Editor's many skills come in handy. The sentences start chunky and clunky; the Editor helps me slim them down and clarify them.

I start with the left hand:

- I study the pros list for the left hand.
- I study the cons list from the right-hand option.

- I use my *Pattern Maker's* skills to come up with a messy, wordy summary of all the important points.
- I use my *Editor's* skills to clean up the wordy summary.

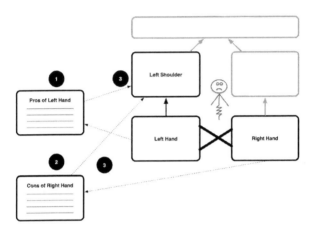

Then I repeat the process for the right-hand side of the cloud.

Note: We want to take the *pros from one hand* and the *cons from the other hand*. Sometimes they're very similar lists, just worded slightly differently. Sometimes there's magic hidden in the other hand's cons list that wouldn't have revealed itself if we had just listed the cons.

CHAPTER 27

FRIENDS 2

When Ross says that Julie is "not Rachel," we all know exactly what he means.

Sorta.

We get the gist, anyway.

But that lovey-dovey sorta language is way too wishy-washy for our friend CorkScrew BoB.

When BoB flips "Julie is not Rachel" on its head, it appears that Ross is simply saying that "Rachel is Rachel."

If we went with that our cloud would look like this:

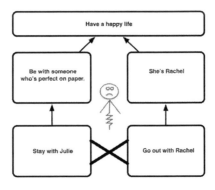

The right shoulder adds nothing.[1]

It certainly doesn't answer the question "What does Ross gain from going out with Rachel?"

Following a consultation with my daughters,[2] they helped me tweak the wording, and I came up with this:

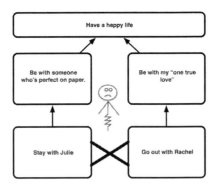

Rachel is 'The One'—his one true love.

He doesn't want to spend the rest of his life with

someone who isn't Rachel, even if she looks perfect on paper.

So, he made his decision: He would break up with Julie. And then his cloud looked something like this.

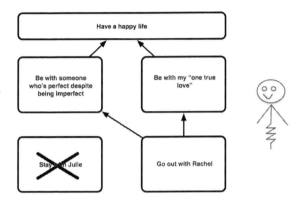

There are no longer two conflicting options because:

- He removed one option (bye Julie),
- He reworded one shoulder, then
- He understood that Rachel gave him the best of both worlds.

His dilemma disappeared.

CHAPTER 28

HARD WORK

W hen we say that we 'draw out' a cloud, we're describing the act of drawing and writing out the cloud diagram.

But that phrase 'draw out' also means to:

- Entice something to come out of hiding.
- Get someone to speak freely.

When you are *UpThinking,* you're having a conversation with yourself and you're trying to entice your deep thoughts and motivations out of hiding.

Sometimes they come out quickly and willingly, but if not, the pros and cons process helps.

Don't be surprised when you come across a cloud where the benefits are hard to articulate.

Keep persevering. Maybe mull over the cloud for a few days. Ask your partner. Or your kids. Or, better still, stop thinking about it and let the 4 friends that live in the back of your brain figure the words out for you.

It's worth it.

You can't resolve your dilemma without knowing the benefits.

And more often than not, the moment you figure them out is also the moment you know exactly what you've gotta do next.

The moment Ross realized Rachel was 'the one' he knew he had to break up with Julie.

That was his tent-pole decision. It was a momentous decision that set the rest of his life in motion.

Unfortunately, there were a few other things he should have done, but didn't.

He didn't destroy the pros and cons list.

He did not destroy the pros and cons list.

He DID NOT destroy the pros and cons list.

Rachel found it.

She discovered that Ross thought she is "spoiled," "ditzy," "too into her looks" and "just a waitress." And also, if those weren't enough, that—ouch—she has "chubby ankles."

Rachel made her decision.

And, instantly, Ross had zero girlfriends.

That was one less girlfriend than he had when the episode started.

And it was two less girlfriends than Joey was suggesting he could have had if Ross had played his cards a little differently.

The show ends with Rachel sitting inside the friends' apartment on a window seat, ignoring Ross who is on the balcony outside looking in while torrential rain pours down on him. It feels like NYC is crying for them.

PART 7

THE SHOULDERS ARE THE KEY

CHAPTER 29

TWO CLOUDS

This section features two very similar-looking, but rather different clouds. The first one took years to fully resolve. And when I finally resolved it, it instantly created the second.

CHAPTER 30

LEPRECHAUNS VS. HOBBITS

I'm from New Zealand. My wife is from Ireland.
They're a long way apart and we could only live in one of them at any one time.

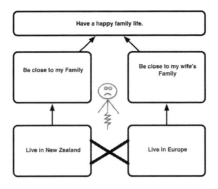

Notice how the alternatives are geographic. They conflict because, as my mother used to say to me when I was a kid, she "couldn't be in two places at one time."

We briefly considered moving to live half-way between

both, in San Francisco, where the flight time between both home countries is far less, but we decided that the compromise would have meant we had far less total time with our families.

Georgie's pinecone vs food cloud was also geographic, and like that conflict, we resolved this dilemma by adding the word 'LATER' to the left-hand option, and adding the word 'NOW' to the right-hand option.

That is, our tent-pole decisions were that:

- We'd Live in Europe NOW, and
- Move to New Zealand LATER.

We made four new supporting decisions:

- We would use our savings and vacation time to travel to New Zealand most years.
- Although we couldn't physically be in two places at one time, our images and voices could be, so we did our best to make phone calls, then Skype calls, then FaceTime calls.
- We'd ask my family to travel to visit us, whenever they could, and
- We decided that we would move to New Zealand when the time was right.

This dilemma was for me, my wife, our kids, and our extended families easily as important as Churchill's Coal vs Oil Dilemma was to him.

———

IN LATE 2016, we knew the time was right to move to New Zealand as my Mum got very sick.

We didn't know what would happen to her, or how my dad would cope if things got worse, but we decided to move to New Zealand.

My wife and I immediately quit our jobs, put our house on the market, and told our kids that we were moving. Somehow during that conversation with our kids, amidst the tears, I promised that we'd get a dog when we moved to New Zealand. That dog turned out to be Georgie.

To paraphrase a line from The West Wing TV show: my wife and I decided to jump off a cliff together and hold hands on the way down while we figured out where we were going to live.

CHAPTER 31

A TALE OF TWO CITIES

(B efore you read on: my mum recovered, thankfully.)
Once we had decided to move to New Zealand,
we had to decide where in New Zealand we wanted to live.
There were two candidates:

- Wellington, NZ's capital city, and one of the
  coolest little cities in the world. I lived there in
  my 20s and I loved it. We had friends there and
  it'd be easy for me to find work.
- Nelson, my hometown, where my parents and
  siblings live. It's one of NZ's sunniest regions
  with loadsa beaches, restaurants and it's a great
  place for kids to grow up. It also has a lot of
  modern necessities i.e., electricity, a good book
  shop, and surprisingly fast internet access. The
  one thing it doesn't have: work for people
  like me.

The problem:

- Wellington is at the south of NZ's North Island.

- Nelson is in the northern part of the South Island.
- It's a 6+ hour ferry and car trip, or an expensive 30-minute flight to get between the two.

You see the two conflicting options—the hands—right?

We were torn between living in Wellington and living in Nelson.

Like this:

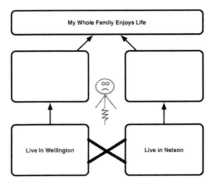

And the pros and cons of each?

That's easy:

- My wife and I would both easily find work in Wellington, so we could afford to live well, but it wasn't really where we wanted to live.
- But Nelson is a beautiful place to live and that's where my parents were (which was the driver of our move). But there's no work there for people like me.

Our cloud looked something like this:

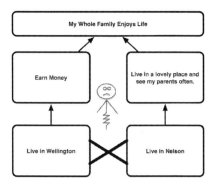

It looks simple and harmless, right?

The reality is it caused me a huge amount of stress and anxiety.

Can you imagine the thoughts pinballing around inside my head?

We have to live in Wellington otherwise we will be broke. But the whole point of moving back to NZ was to be near my parents and we can't do that if we're living in Wellington. We will only be able to visit them every few months. We'll spend all of our time and money flying over to Nelson. That's not cheap when there are 4 of us. And it'll be tiring. It'd be so much better if we were in Nelson. But if we do that we will have no money coming in. What are we

going to do, live under a bridge?
Maybe we could live with our parents.
WHAT? I'd rather live under a bridge.

And so on.

All of this was happening while I was worried about my mum and dad. And my wife and kids were upset because while I was moving home at long last, they were being wrenched away from their friends and family to the other side of the world.

CHAPTER 32

BEST OF BOTH

O nce you've drawn out your cloud, the next question
is: 'What would BoB do next?'

CorkScrew BoB would figure out how to get **the best
of both worlds**.

That's his thing. His trick. BoB stands for **Best of
Both** . . . remember?

He would tell us to pick one side—say Wellington—
then ask how we could live in Wellington AND ALSO get
the benefits of living in Nelson.

Like this:

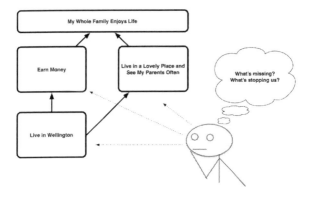

Specifically, he'd ask to answer this:

What would we need to do to have a great time living and working in Wellington AND also see my parents often?

There are a couple of more generic prompts that help:

1. *What's stopping you from getting the best of both worlds?*
2. *What's missing which, if you could get it, would let you do both?*

BoB would then ask us to swap sides, and ask:

What would we need to do to earn enough money to live in Nelson?

What's stopping you from getting the best of both worlds?

What's missing which, if you could get it, would let you do both?

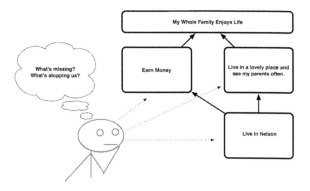

I have answered these questions for both sides, but I'm not going to share them here.

That's partly because the lists are soooooooo BOOOORING.

Zzzzzzzzz.

But mostly it's because I'd rather tell you how I resolved this dilemma in real life.

In real life, I was too close to the dilemma and so stressed I couldn't think clearly.

So, I hired a coach to help me.

CHAPTER 33

TEN OUT OF TEN

My coach's name is Antoinette[1] and here's how things went:

1. In our second session, Antoinette asked me to close my eyes and describe what the "10 out of 10 version of your return home looks like."
2. I closed my eyes then started speaking.
3. I had no idea what would come out . . .
4. I said, "Well, obviously, we'd move to Wellington, the capital city. That's where the work is. I'll get a job there no problem. And so will my wife."
5. "And, since we've already got a few very good friends there, it's not like we'll be starting entirely fresh."
6. "I'll be able to go bike riding again, like when I lived there during my 20s . . . Except, of course, back then I was single, and I lived on the flat. Now I've got a family, we'd almost certainly have to live up in the hills. It's not so easy cycling when you live up in the hills."

7. "We'll visit my parents more often. That's why we're moving back. They live in Nelson, in the South Island, across the Cook Strait. It'll be expensive for all 4 of us to fly to there, of course, but we'll probably go back once every 2, 3 or 4 months."

8. I must have frowned . . .

9. . . . because Antoinette said, "Stop."

10. I opened my eyes.

11. "That doesn't sound like a 10 out of 10."

12. I thought a moment. "No, it doesn't."

13. She said, "It sounds more like 6 out of 10."

14. I nodded. She was right. She was definitely right.

15. I'd instantly compromised . . . without even realizing it.

16. I'd gone for the 'easy' solution because . . . because, well, it seemed possible.

17. Antoinette said, "Close your eyes and start again."

18. I closed my eyes and started again, but this time I didn't compromise.

19. I went for the real 10 out of 10.

20. "We'll move to Nelson, which is where I grew up. It's lovely there. Sunny, most of the year. We can even have BBQs in the middle of winter—if we want."

21. "And we can go swimming in the sea from November through April. The girls will love that."

22. "It's a great place for cycling, all year round, too."

23. "My parents live in Nelson, so we can see them every week. The kids will especially love that."

24. "And we can spend time with my brother and my sister and their families too."
25. "But . . ." I said, realizing this 10 out of 10 wasn't the easy option, ". . . I'll still need to work."
26. Presented with an obstacle, I set about solving it.
27. "I can work in Wellington. It's an easy 30-minute flight."
28. I grimaced.
29. I didn't want to be working away 5 days a week
30. So, presented with another obstacle, I set about solving it.
31. "I'll need to figure out how to work away 2 or 3 days a week, and still make enough money to live."
32. I nodded to myself. That thought transformed the obstacle from a problem into a challenge.
33. "We could live very frugally. Or I could figure out how to earn more money . . ."
34. Hmm . . .
35. I knew the secret to earning more money was having something scarce, that others wanted or needed, and being able to sell it.
36. I had the scarce stuff.
37. But—this is another obstacle—I wasn't good at selling myself.
38. I'd never learned how.
39. I said, 'I'll need to figure out how to feel comfortable selling myself. I'll need to figure out how to charge fees that reflect the value I deliver, not the hours I work."
40. Hmmm . . .
41. I said, "And, I can do that."

42. I opened my eyes then looked at Antoinette and smiled.

43. She smiled back, "That sounds much more like a 10 out of 10."

44. I nodded. It did.

CHAPTER 34

DON'T COMPROMISE

Did you notice how quickly I compromised and treated the easiest option—Wellington—as if it was the 10-out-of-10 option?

I picked the *easy option* (Wellington) and tried to make it better—moving it from a 6 to a 7, then perhaps an 8.

I should have picked the best option (Nelson, my 10 out of 10) and worked on making it real.

I should have picked sides, but just to get me started.

Nowadays, as soon as you're happy with your cloud, CorkScrew BoB makes a habit of asking:

Of the two alternatives, do you have a preference?

And, if you do, he uses the 'what's stopping you?' and 'what's missing?' questions to help you figure out how to make it real.

Answering the 'what's stopping you?' question creates a brief list of obstacles or hurdles that you have to overcome.

Answering the 'what's missing?' question creates a brief list of gaps that you need to fill.

For me, the key obstacle that was stopping me from moving to Nelson was that there was no work for people like me there. I overcame that obstacle by deciding I would travel for work. But I didn't know how to sell myself at high rates, which was a skills gap that was surprisingly easy to fill.

You'll usually find one or two obstacles or gaps that are trickier to tackle than the others, so you'll focus on them. You'll find a bunch of easier obstacles and gaps, and you'll sort them out over time.

————

SHORTLY AFTER MY session with Antoinette, I stumbled across a comment from Cal Newport, author of the book *Deep Work*.

I can't find it now, but it went something like this:

Most people choose their work, then build their life around that.

Some people choose their life, then build their work around that.

That is the best advice I've ever read and it is exactly what I did.

My tent pole decision was to live with my family in Nelson then travel away to work 3 days a week.

In order to make that work, I had to take a few other actions:

- I had to learn how to earn more money by selling myself at higher rates.
- I had to figure out how to sell and deliver my work from Nelson without needing to travel. (I now do this full time).

So that's how my family and I got the best of both worlds.

The saddest and best part of our move was that my dad

passed away unexpectedly a couple of years after we moved back. I'm glad I got to spend two years with him, going fishing with him, seeing him every week, which I wouldn't if we'd stayed in Scotland or moved to Wellington.

Here's the cloud now:

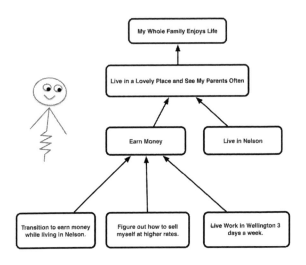

Notice how I moved things around a bit, so it no longer looks like the standard cloud shape. That's okay.

PART 8

CRACKING CLOUDS

CHAPTER 35

EGGS ARE BOTH STRONG AND FRAGILE

R ight, now I've got a quirky job for you to do:

1. Go to your kitchen and grab an egg.
2. Go stand in front of your sink.
3. Now, with the egg gently held in the palm of your hand, even more gently close your fingers around the egg, as if you're providing a protective wrapper.
4. Now squeeze the egg tightly, making sure to apply the pressure evenly around the egg.

Did the egg break?

According to the internet, it shouldn't have. (And, if it did . . . I'm so sorry . . . please go wash your hands and pretend the egg didn't break. Or, let me know and I'll email you a new egg.)

Eggs are both fragile and strong, at the same time.

Their eggy shape makes them strong, in much the same way that an arch supports a bridge, and their roundness distributes the pressure evenly around the shell rather than concentrating it at any one point.

Dilemmas are like that too. The tension inherent in their structure holds them together. That tension is the pull between the two alternatives; the 'diametrically opposed' options. So long as that conflict exists, the dilemma exists.

Now, can I ask you to please imagine for me a little tiny duckling—a real one—that hasn't hatched yet and is still inside an egg. Mummy Duck has been sitting on the egg and it's been strong enough to support her weight all this time, but now the little, tiny duckling needs to break out.

What does the duckling do to escape?

What's its trick?

The little duckling pecks and pecks at a single point, until the egg cracks.

It's much the same when you need to crack a dilemma, a cloud. You have to keep chipping away at it until it cracks.

Finally, the best piece of cloud-cracking advice I can give you is this: it's always easier to solve someone else's problems than it is your own, so go ask someone else.

CHAPTER 36

THREE WEAK POINTS

H ere's the good news.
  Clouds have three weak points that are particularly vulnerable:

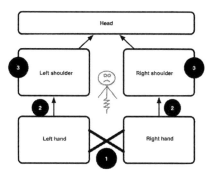

1. The big **X**—that sits between the two hands.
2. The arrows connecting the shoulder and the hand (also known as 'the arms').
3. The wording of the shoulders.

And—here's the secret—to break the conflict all you have to do (initially) is rewrite the words and perhaps add a few more textboxes and arrows to the diagram.

Remember: EDITing is editing.

CHAPTER 37

THE CONFLICT X

ow can you rewrite the cloud so you can do both hands, without conflict?

H You've seen a few examples of this already.

- Churchill only converted his warships to be oil, so on one hand he had oil-powered warships, and on the other hand, he had coal-powered ships too.
- Georgie added the words 'now' on one 'hand' and 'later' to the other 'hand' on her pinecone and food cloud to get the best of both.
- I realized I could easily change the words on each hand so that I 'use Roam Research for purpose A' and 'use Notion for purpose B', so there was no longer a conflict ($\mathbf{X}$) and I didn't need to choose between them.
- Churchill drank champagne (and reputedly other drinks) in the bath because he didn't care one iota what other people thought. He removed the $\mathbf{X}$ from the diagram and said, "I shall do both."

Sometimes you might realize you're missing something —time, money, knowledge, or a particular skill—that would allow you to have both options.

For instance, you can 'have your cake and eat it too' if you have the time and money to buy, or bake more cake.

You'll find these prompts useful:

- *What's stopping me from doing both?*
- *What's missing that would allow me to do both?*

And if those questions don't help, ask yourself:

- *Why on earth do these two options conflict with each other?*
- *Why on earth can't I have both?*

Answer the prompt questions then read each answer out loud, then, using your most dismissive and cynical voice, say, "Pah! That's only true if . . ." and see what comes out.

CHAPTER 38

THE ARMS

You know that:

- You want both of the benefits sitting on BoB's shoulders.
- You can't have them both so long as the two options conflict.

If you were to chop off BoB's left hand and replace it with a new hand (perhaps a bionic hand) that gives you the benefits written on his left shoulder, your conflict would disappear.

I did this with my Nelson vs. Wellington dilemma. I chose to keep the "Live in Nelson" option and remove the "Live in Wellington" option. If I'd have left it at that I would have no income, so I replaced it with a new hand; I found a way to earn money while living in Nelson.

When you read from the shoulders down to the hands, you use this template:

"In order to (shoulder), I MUST (hand)."

The word "MUST" implies the action is the only way to get the benefit sitting on the shoulder.

Often, it's not. As that old saying goes, there are many ways to skin a cat.

In order to "Earn Money," I MUST "Live in Wellington."

- Must I really?
- Isn't there another way to get the same benefit?

It's helpful to think of the two hands as being options, not solutions.

Now try adding the word 'because' to the end of the template:

"In order to (shoulder), I MUST (hand) because . . ."

When you do this, force your *Why Maker* to list out as many reasons as it can think of.

And then, using your most cynical, dismissive voice again, run through the list asking, "Really? Are you sure?"

CHAPTER 39

REWORD THE SHOULDERS

This one's magic!

Sometimes, once you've got your cloud drawn out and discovered a few clever new options that feel like they've cracked the cloud, you'll feel a little uneasy.

That might mean you have found your tent pole changes but still need a few more supporting changes.

Alternatively, the shoulders might need a little rewording.

I did that with Ross's Cloud, when he changed "Be with someone who's perfect" to "Be with someone who's perfect despite being imperfect."

The words on the cloud didn't exist until you drew them out.

They're your words.

Edit them until they feel right.

CHAPTER 40

BONUS

Here's a little bonus trick.

A friend of mine, Rory Sutherland, author of the wonderful book, *Alchemy*, has a very counterintuitive rule:

Sometimes the opposite of a good idea . . . is also a good idea.

You might find that your cloud represents two good ideas, but you prefer the first good idea and your preference is biasing you away from the new good idea.

To put that another way: the alternative idea might be a lot better than you think.

So open your mind, then go see if that's true.

You may be surprised what you find.

PART 9

PRACTICALITIES

CHAPTER 41

THERE ARE MANY WAYS TO DRAW A CLOUD

A cloud, as you know, is made up of 5 distinct chunks of text.

So long as you understand the relationship between the 5 chunks of text, you can draw, type, remember, store them in as few or as many different formats and media as you like.

You can put them on sticky notes.

Pick what suits you and the people you're working with.

Pick whatever works best at the time.

Here're some examples of real-world clouds in different formats.

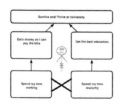

THIS FORMAT IS the format I use for this and other books.

I use a drawing package called OmniGraffle. It works on my iPad and my Mac, and it exports high-quality images that work well with publishing platforms.

Apple's Keynote and Microsoft's PowerPoint produce nice-looking graphics and are quick and easy to use too.

———

Clouds can be drawn horizontally or vertically.

The traditional format I learned is horizontal.

I prefer the vertical format.

It doesn't matter which format you use.

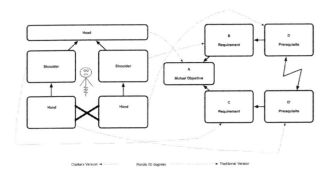

MINDMAP

Sometimes I do my thinking in the MindNode app on my iPhone, iPad and Mac. Here's a MindNode cloud where I've set the layout option to vertical:

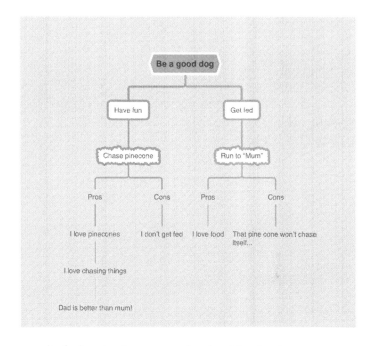

And, here's the same cloud with the layout set to horizontal.

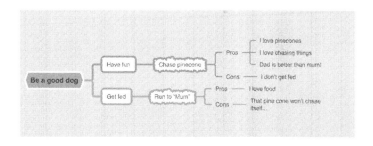

As you draw or type your clouds, focus on getting the words out of your head. Don't worry about getting the spelling or grammar correct ... unless you can't help yourself.

I like thinking with my fingertips and I've grown to love the outlining tool, *Roam Research*.

Here's a cloud I typed up inside Roam, while I was debating whether I should use Roam or its competitor Notion.

- Mission: have a good way to think with my fingertips,
- **Left-hand: use roam**
- **left shoulder**: roam is simpler (now that I've gotten the hang of it)
  - **pros:**
    - I find it easy to type in this - it just feels more natural
    - I've learnt most of the tricky bits - enough to get me going
    - keeps growing
  - **cons**
    - it's quite pricey (for an app)
    - it's still evolving ... not fully formed
- **Left-hand: use notion**
- **right shoulder**: bigger, all round solution
  - mobile apps
  - better infrastructure
  - big, successful product
  - free
  - will probably adopt roams best bits over time (already started)

Here's the same cloud but with the pros and cons "folded" away so it looks less cluttered.

- Mission: have a good way to think with my fingertips,
- **Left-hand: use roam**
- **left shoulder**: roam is simpler (now that I've gotten the hang of it)
- **Left-hand: use notion**
- **right shoulder**: bigger, all round solution

I wanted to use one tool, but then, after drawing the cloud out, I realized that I could use both, but for different things, and that's what I do.

PAPER

Sometimes nothing beats paper.

Here's an incomplete and incorrect cloud I found earlier.

It was hidden in a folder I used while writing this book.

I have terrible handwriting so don't try to read it. If you do try to read it, you'll notice that the right-hand shoulder is nonsense. That's okay, because 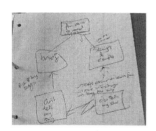 the cloud disappeared the moment I wrote the word "brief" on the left-hand shoulder.

I was trying to figure out if I should use stories in this book. I'd spent weeks with ducklings whisper in one ear, "Use stories because they're easier to read" and other ducklings whispering in the other ear, "Yeah, but stories can go on a bit."

Writing the word 'brief' shut both lots of ducklings up, and let me get on with writing.

———

WHITEBOARDS

Here's a photo of a cloud drawn on a real physical whiteboard.

I've no idea when this was taken, what we were talking about, or even which country we were in.

Same with this:

Ditto this:

Whiteboards are great when working with others (in person).

ELECTRONIC WHITEBOARD

And here's a screenshot of a cloud I helped a client draw using the online collaboration and white-boarding tool, Miro.

It's the online equivalent of using sticky notes on a Flipchart.

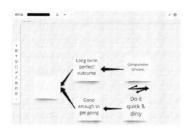

USE YOUR HANDS, SHOULDERS

Finally, if you find yourself trying to create a cloud in a situation where you can't write, draw or type—perhaps because you're driving—try placing the words on your actual hands, your shoulders and your head.

I bet you already use physical gestures with your hands like Ross did, when you explain to someone that "on the one hand" you could X, but "on the other hand" you could Y.

Once you realize you're already doing that, adding the shoulders is a no-brainer.

You can add the head too . . . but it's usually not necessary.

CHAPTER 42

VENN AND 2X2 – DON'T SHOW YOUR WORKING

Put yourself in Churchill's shoes.

Imagine that you have just worked through the cloud process and come up with this splendid-looking cloud.

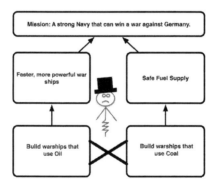

You've even figured out a particularly audacious solution.

And now you need to persuade your Prime Minister to spend a fortune.

It's the only way you can win the war.

Here's my tip: Don't show the Prime Minister the cloud.

Instead, show the PM the conclusions of your cloud but in a more familiar format.

Like this 2x2 matrix:

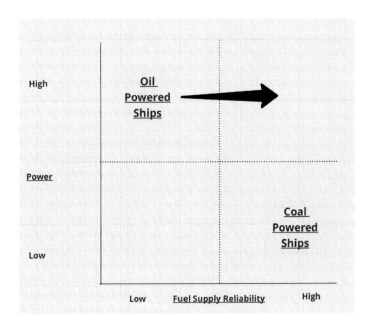

You want your PM's attention focused on solving the dilemma, not the weird-looking diagram.

I remember when I used to do mathematics exams and they'd tell us to "show your working" as well as your final answer. It's okay to use the cloud to do your working, not show it, and show your results in a different (more familiar) format.[1]

You might prefer to use a Venn Diagram, like this:

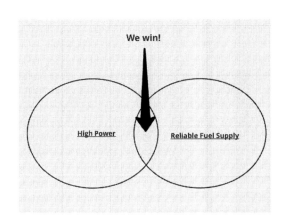

CHAPTER 43

SPOTTING CLOUDS

Y ou know how to draw out clouds. You know how to crack them. But how do you know you're facing a dilemma?

How do you know it's time to use the cloud and EDIT process?

The short answer:

- Look out for situations where you have to make a choice between two alternatives, and the choice is not easy.
- If the choice is easy, you don't face a dilemma.
- If the choice is tricky, maybe you do.

Often, dilemmas and conflicts jump up and jab you in the nose. You'll recognize them when you use, or hear other people use phrases like:

- "I'm torn . . ."
- "There's a tension between . . ."
- "I'm conflicted . . ."
- "I have a dilemma" or

- "I'm stuck."

Other times, they'll hide, and you'll have to go looking for them.

Where do you look?

Inside your brain.

If your brain is distracted with recurrent killer ducklings and problem-pinball then that's your brain's way of telling you there's a problem, and the way you've been tackling it so far hasn't worked.

That's when you draw a cloud. And you do that by identifying two choices that seem to conflict.

———

THANK'S to the *Pattern Maker* you get better and better at spotting clouds over time.

The good news is that you've just studied a bunch of clouds, so you've already done most of the hard work.

PART 10

CORKSCREW MINDS

CHAPTER 44

WRAP UP

When you ask creative people how they did something, they feel a little guilty because they didn't really do it, they just saw something. It seemed obvious to them after a while. That's because they were able to connect experiences they've had and synthesize new things.

Steve Jobs – from *I, Steve: Steve Jobs in His Own Words*

In the early days of World War Two, shortly after Churchill became Prime Minister, he created a handful of secret units staffed by people he described as having 'corkscrew minds.'

You may have seen movies about them: "The Monument Men," "The Imitation Game" and "Die Hard IV."

Maybe you've read about Operation Mincemeat's brilliant D-Day deceptions (or maybe you'll have to Google it).

Churchill's head of Naval Intelligence, Admiral John

Godfrey,[1] claimed that having a 'corkscrew mind' was the essential skill of espionage work, it was "the ability to understand how other men think, and then think differently."

CorkScrew BoB is named after these CorkScrew Thinkers.

(It's a fortunate coincidence that he looks like a corkscrew.)

But don't be mistaken: BoB doesn't have a CorkScrew Mind.

He doesn't have a mind.

He's an imaginary corkscrew-shaped stick figure.

What BoB does have is:

- A diagram,
- A process for filling out that diagram, and,
- Two tricks.

And BoB has an attitude.

He does not want you to get hung up on rules. He does want you to get the gist of the EDIT process. He doesn't want you to draw the prettiest and perfectest diagrams in the whole wide world. He wants you to seek out the "Best of Both" Worlds.

And, finally, BoB has an email address.

He set it up to resolve a dilemma he and I had:

- I wanted to keep this book as short as possible.
- He wanted to add more example clouds and tips into the book and make it bigger.

I wouldn't budge, so he set up an email account.

If you email him at bob@corkscrew.solutions and say "hello," he will send you more stories about corkscrew thinkers—people like Bruce Springsteen, Barack Obama, President FDR, and Miley Cyrus (yes, Miley Cyrus). One day he might even tell you the real reason he's called Cork-Screw BoB.

8. ELI GOLDRATT

1. You get extra points if you spot the spelling mistake.

24. THE PATTERN MAKER, THE EDITOR AND THE WHY FINDER

1. The Librarian is unreliable and makes up stuff. The Pattern Maker dreams up stuff and is easily distracted. And, as you well know, you don't ever want to invite The Editor to a party.

25. FRIENDS 2

1. Ross was in interesting company. Bill Gates made a pros and cons list for marriage before proposing to Melinda Gates. We don't know what was in the list, but when Charles Darwin did the same, his pros list included 'constant companion,' 'charms of music & female chit-chat' and the cons list included 'means limited,' 'no books' and 'terrible loss of time.'

26. UPTHINKING – PROS AND CONS QUESTIONS

1. Option: Switch to Oil
   Pros:
   Powerful ships.
   Smaller ships.
   Longer voyages.
   Equal or better than enemy's ships.
   Etc.
   Cons:
   Coal mine owners will be angry.
   It's a long risky trip from Persia to England.
   Our supplier could stop selling fuel to us and sell it to the enemy.
   We could end up in a bidding war and the price of oil will soar.

We could end up with our ships stuck in harbor, or at sea.
The enemy will dominate the seas.
Option: Stick with Coal
Pros:
Safe, secure fuel source.
Ships at sea for longer (because they don't run out of fuel).
Cons:
Our enemy will have faster, more powerful ships.
We will lose many battles.

27. FRIENDS 2

1. It's a bit like asking a teenager why they need $20 and they say, "Coz."
2. The consultation cost me $20.

33. TEN OUT OF TEN

1. Find her on Twitter at @acvross. She is FANTASTIC.

42. VENN AND 2X2 – DON'T SHOW YOUR WORKING

1. Don't tell anyone, but these days, now that I'm very proficient with clouds, I often skip them and go straight to the 2x2 matrix format.

44. WRAP UP

1. And also the boss of Ian Fleming—the creator of James Bond.

Printed in Great Britain
by Amazon

72689623R00090